Sistership

A KEEPSAKE Journal

Sistership

A KEEPSAKE Journal

ANDREA M. BROOKS

Kravitz and Sons LLC
204 E Arlington Blvd. Suite B
Greenville, NC 27858

Published by Kravitz and Sons LLC.

ISBN: 979-8-89639-665-9 (sc)
ISBN: 979-8-89639-664-2 (e)

Library of Congress Control Number: TO FOLLOW

Dedication

I dedicate this book to girlfriends, friends, and Sistah-friends everywhere! To my twin sons Charles Lee and Andrew Ra'Shad, my grandloves Ava Grace and Treydan, may you always know the power of a loving friendship and always cherish your friends.

In Loving Memory of my grandmother's Charlotte Rosier and Neather Belle-Ferrell, your strength and courage lives through me every day, thank you!

Acknowledgements

Sistership is a journal for Girlfriend's Everywhere. Especially for my sister-friends who I could not imagine my life without: Kim Banks-Patton, Dr. Yvonne Terrell-Powell, Kikora Dorsey, Carmella Frazier, In Loving Memory of Jocelyn "Queen" Myres, what a blessing you've all been to my life, all the countless moments we have shared will never be forgotten. Continue to live "victorious" lives. May God Continue to Bless you All Richly!

Thank You's!

My Parents Kelly (RIH) & Ruth Easter who taught me the meaning of sharing and caring for others. My father Lucious Boone, Jr. My sisters Antionette Easter, and Chrishenda Cooper, MaryAnn Davis, thanks for your love & continuous support. Special thanks to my Auntie Rosa Walker for always supporting and believing in me, Irma Patzel RIH, Rosalyn Walker, Kyendra Williams-Jackson (daughter in-love) DiJanna Honable, Regina Chatman-Henderson, Michele Gipson, Edelweiss Austria, Tammy Clay-Jones, Tamisha Birgman, Tanya Hart, Rolanda Carriere, Karin Crews-Powers, Kerry Zeida, Desiree Brown, Valerie Hill, Sherry Boyland, LaRenda Myres, Nia Steward, Katrice "KB" Barfield, Lacharl "LaLa" Carter, Camile "Alize" Robertson, Julie "Doll" Scroggs, Ava Isreal Anderson, Sharron Anderson, Star Johnson, Melanie Matkin, "RF", To my Tallahassee & Sopchoppy Florida Family, and the Brooks Family thank you for always believing and loving me! It has taken a circle of love to achieve……………… My nieces: Alexandria Ruth, Avonna (RIH 4.17.2026), Nyayha Hunni, Nephews: Christopher, Kelly, Jonathan, Joshua, Alexander. In Memory of my brother Corde' Air De Coure' "CA", 2.5.2002.

In life, if we're slightly lucky, we crossed the path of a "sistah friend" that we just have a natural connection with. In my life, I have been blessed to have some special "sistah-friends", and when I say the word friend I mean friend. There is a distinction between acquaintances, people you know, and the people I would call my friend. I know I am blessed because of course I think my friends are the "crème of the crop". They are smart, witty, happy, unique and, for the most part, fulfilled. I love them all dearly. Sometimes, I literally talk to them all day—because after hanging up with one, I somehow end up speaking to the others. Two of them recently relocated to other states, and I was devastated! I eventually got over it, realizing it was not the end of the world, and that I wasn't going to die—I was actually a phone call or plane ride away. At that point, I also realized that real friendship can stand the test of time and distance. I worried about whether our friendship would last. Would my friends meet others who might phase me out of their lives? Well, that didn't happen. We communicate weekly, if not daily. Our time apart has also been special—the anticipation of waiting for the mailman to deliver letters or packages from Federal Express is actually fun! And goodness, if we miss a delivery, all hell breaks loose.

Despite the challenges, we have become a new class of "managed-care" sistahs.

Friendship is based on trust and respect, and it's a revolving door (it works both ways). Once trust is tampered with you may never get back what you once shared, and I believe trust is the key to any relationship! Of course you'll always have the group of wanta-be-friends! Who mean you no good! Those "haters" that get into your business and you hear it all over town.

Friends are vital; they provide a sense of belonging—a place in your heart and in your life that is just for them. If you've been blessed with friendships like mine, you simply could not imagine your life without your girlfriends. However, I believe you must develop your own life! And certainly you must know your destiny and be able to stand on your own two-feet. Of course your friends are there to support you not carry you. Building new friendships can often be difficult, and scary because it's means the beginning of sharing your life with someone new. That requires "trust", and in these days and times it's hard to trust. It seems everybody has a motive, and it's better to be safe than sorry. For me, some of the most challenging times of my girlfriendship have been when I needed support while trying to find balance in my professional life and finding out just what direction my life is going! These were particular times I wish I had all my girlfriends actually present not communicating by phone call or email. There are just moments when you need her in your presence. However, regardless of our geographic locations, I know I can always count on them. And when all get together, we have the time of our lives, making new memories.

Girlfriends! People may come and go, and they certainly will, but a true friend will always be there for you no matter what. So, if you've been blessed to have a girlfriend(s), count your blessings.

Our Sistership

To Know You Is To Love You

When we met:

Girlfriends are wonderful we share a great deal of our lives together! You love something particular about them. Let's record some of those things:

I Knew We Would Become the Best of Friends When

Was it something she said or did? Was it her style, grace & beauty?

What Captured Me about you From the Very Start?

A quality or qualities your girlfriend(s) has that stands out. You noticed these attributes about her when you first met.

I Knew We Had the Friendship Connection When

Sometimes situations and circumstances bring people together. Share how your friendship connected:

Lessons I Have Learned From Our Friendship

One of Our Most Memorable Times Was When

Some say that vacation, the party that seemed endless, Girls night out! Our times together always produces a memory, but if I had to choose..........

Only You Could Even Began to Comprehend

Now, I have done some crazy things and lord knows most would not understand. But, when I share it with you, there is a sense of understanding. Girlfriends may not agree but they know what drove you to that point! Remember when:

No Dignity, No Pride and No Morals

Maybe it's one of those scandalous outfits! You never know what to expect next? Girlfriend will try just about anything! She just simply doesn't care at times; let's record a moment(s) I cannot let you forget:

Spirituality

Watching you grow in your spirituality has been wonderful. You are a spiritual inspiration to my spirituality and growth. I recognize through spiritual growth:

Proud Moments I Have Shared With You

Your accomplishments have made me so proud of you. Some proud moment I've shared with you were:

Our Children

It Takes a Village to raise a Child. Having girlfriends to communicate my parenting challenges, and experiences, with has truly been a blessing. I have valued having you in my life to share with. One time in particular was:

A Laugh We'll Never Forget
(Photo Page)

Unconditional Understanding

You never look or expect anything in return. Your ears are always open and your heart is big enough for me.

Birthdays! A Lifetime of Celebrations

The parties are endless the preparation requires your touch and mine! To share our special day as we grow older makes the celebration greater. I couldn't imagine my special day without you! One birthday celebration particularly was:

My Soul Looks Back and Wonders

With special friends by your side, you feel as though you can concur the world. You often wonder how you made it to this point and managed to remain sane...........

Remember When

These are some times I will never forget, and I don't want you to either:

Nothing Ventured, Nothing Gained

Goal setting is very important and sometimes you need that boost or nudge! Realizing that if you don't try you'll never know if you would have succeeded. Your dream became a reality when:

Then & Now
(Photo Page)

Hey! We know everybody changes over time. We may not be able to squeeze into those size "2" slacks anymore! Nor, may our hairstyles flow as they did at one time. Find happiness within yourself, your size, and your overall personal appearance. "You better work it girl".

Destiny

Having you in my life has encouraged me to reach for my destiny and go for it! Let's record some of those achievements:

Thank You!

Thank you for never changing and being there for me whenever I have needed you. I realize I have bent your ear off with all my drama but I really appreciate the comfort I feel in sharing with you. You're not judgmental. You are a precious jewel I found. Thanks for:

Our Similarities

Your Encouragement during Discouraging Times

Girl's Night Out!
(Photo Page)

I'd Like to Share This With You

To me you are such a "diva". I think you will succeed in reaching the goals you set for yourself. You have self- determination and a strong will. With Christ all things are possible.

Some of our Favorite Things

We are friends and we are different, and respecting differences is a large part of staying in healthy friendships! We are each are own person let's check out some of the things we like.

	Mine	**Yours**
Color:		
Book:		
Munches:		
Restaurant:		
Male Vocalist:		
Female Vocalist:		
Song:		
Flower:		
Designer:		
Department Store:		
Spa:		
Movie:		
Get Away:		
Poet:		

Dislikes

One of the benefits of having a Girlfriend is to share your displeasure's with, and I hold absolutely nothing back when I don't like something. You usually know when I am about to "react" to certain situations: Let's Address "dislikes"!

Salespeople who: ________________________________

Friends who: ________________________________

Men who: ________________________________

Women who: ________________________________

Hairstylists who: ________________________________

Groupies who: ________________________________

Family members who: ________________________________

Neighbors who: ________________________________

Kids who: ________________________________

Bosses who: ________________________________

Being Honest, Even when it hurts

Despite what you may feel, one of the values of true friendship is honesty! Knowing you can be honest with your girlfriend(s) is important. Knowing she will be honest with you allows you to respect her opinions. Even when it's not what you want to hear, she's tells you...

Whatever you Imagine

I want so much for you, complete fulfillment is one of them, and I know that you will reach that point. "Joy is coming in the morning sistah-girl"!

Should of, would of, could of

Certainly we all have some things if we could do again we would do differently. I should of, would of, could of, just doesn't help us at this point. However, having you in my life has made me realize:

Music that just seem to heal our hearts, and bring a sense of joy to our lives

List a few theme songs: "I'm Every Woman" would be at the top of my list.

My Prayer for You

My daily prayers include you and your family. I pray:

Joy Cometh in the Morning Girl!

Things may not be bright today but hold on girlfriend your day is soon to come! It's all in the timing.

"Just one of Them Days"

My hair might not be combed, my nail may be broken, secured with a band-aid. Girlfriends! Have a way of being in your presence and realizing it's you! Regardless if your in your beauty queen mode yet! She looks beyond that.

You Never Look for or Expect Something in Return

Expectation is something that doesn't exist in girlfriendships, you give mentally, physically and your hands aren't open waiting for something in return. Your spirit is simply giving. For instance:

This Page Is For You Girlfriend

(Please use this page to do whatever you like)

What single words describe true, test of times "Sisterships/Girlfriendships"

** Communication * Trust * Honesty * Nurture * Intimacy*
** Celebration * Men * Ideas * Romance*
** Beginnings * Responsibility *Transition * Joy * Hope*
** Change * Shopping * Endings * Children*
** Love * Family * Ties * Strength * Advice * Growth*
** Tears * Sister * Crisis * History * Source*
** Confide * Home * Laughter * Pain * Loyalty*
** Openness * Values * Morals * Support*
•Connection

Girlfriend
by Andrea M. Brooks

One who makes me feel comfortable,
One who understands me,
One who understand that in life,
something's often keep us from spending
as much time as we'd like together.

But, realizes no matter how far apart we are
nothing could change the closeness
Girlfriend's share.

She understands my needs, sometimes
before I know myself.
She knows from my voice when I am hurting,
or when I'm having a bad day.
She doesn't give it a second thought
in telling me when I'm right or wrong.
She knows when I need advice or encouragement.

Girlfriend Knows

www.ingramcontent.com/pod-product-compliance
Ingram Content Group UK Ltd.
Pitfield, Milton Keynes, MK11 3LW, UK
UKRC032309290726
14090UKWH00004B/406